This book

belongs to

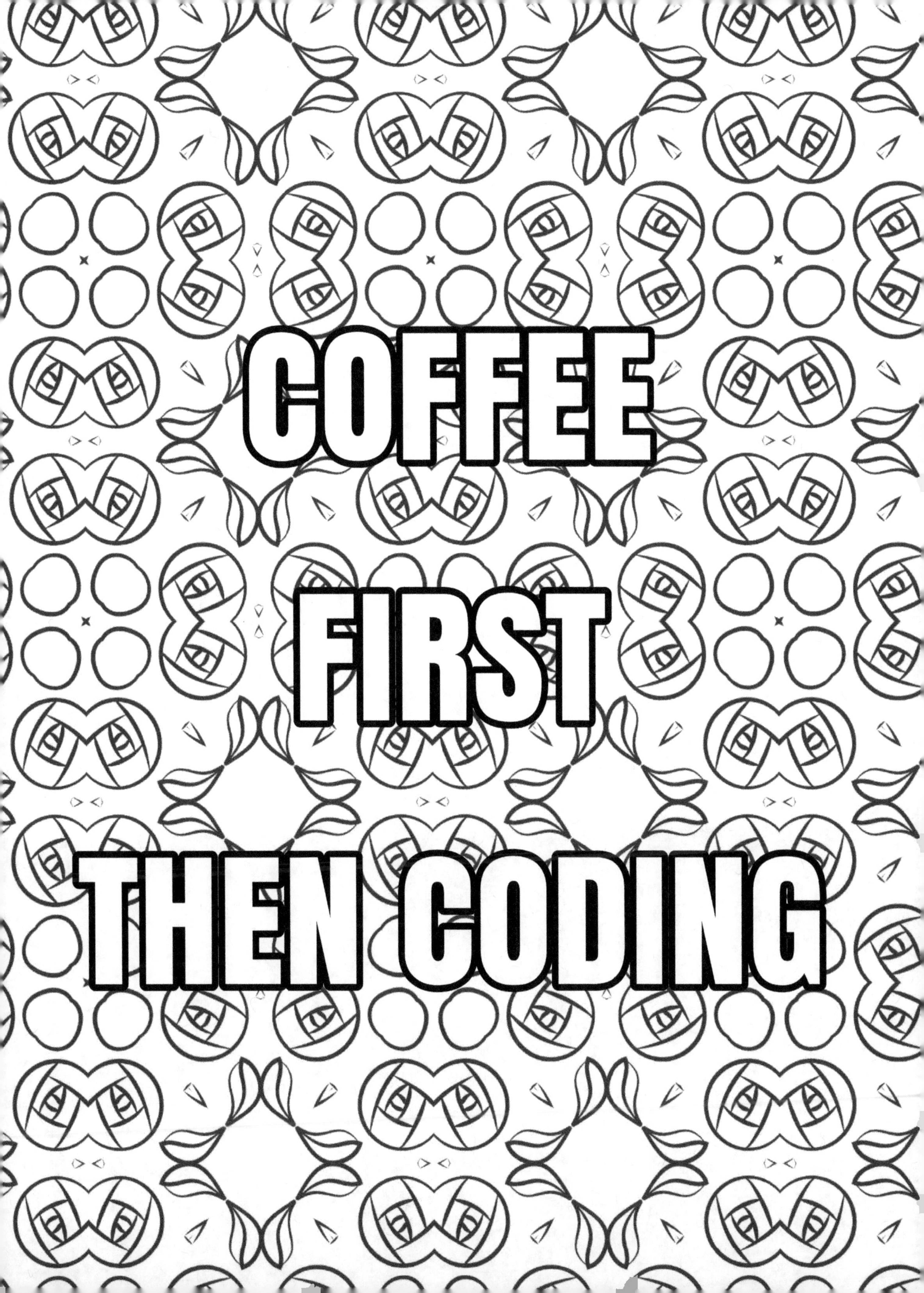
COFFEE
FIRST
THEN CODING

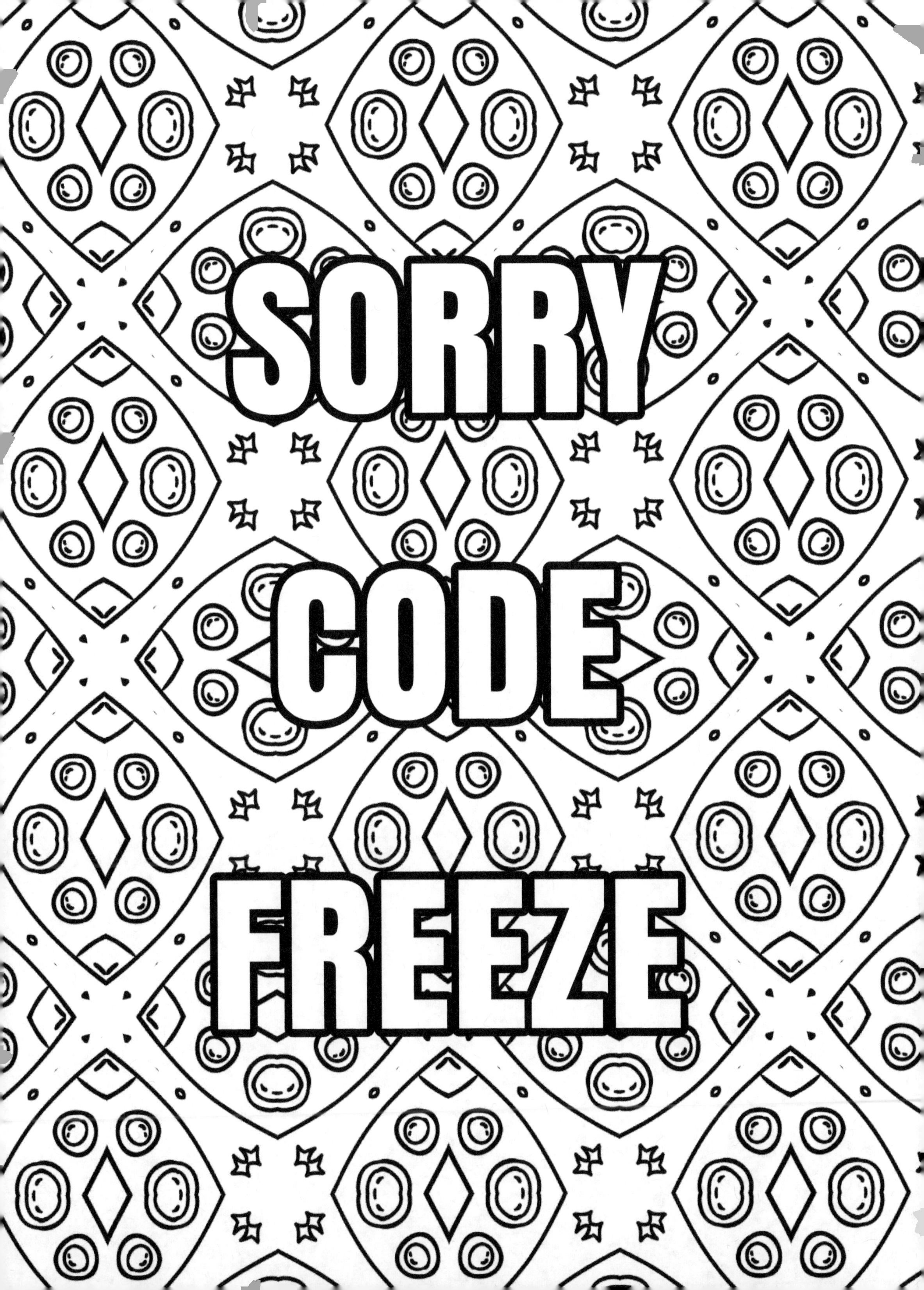
SORRY
CODE
FREEZE

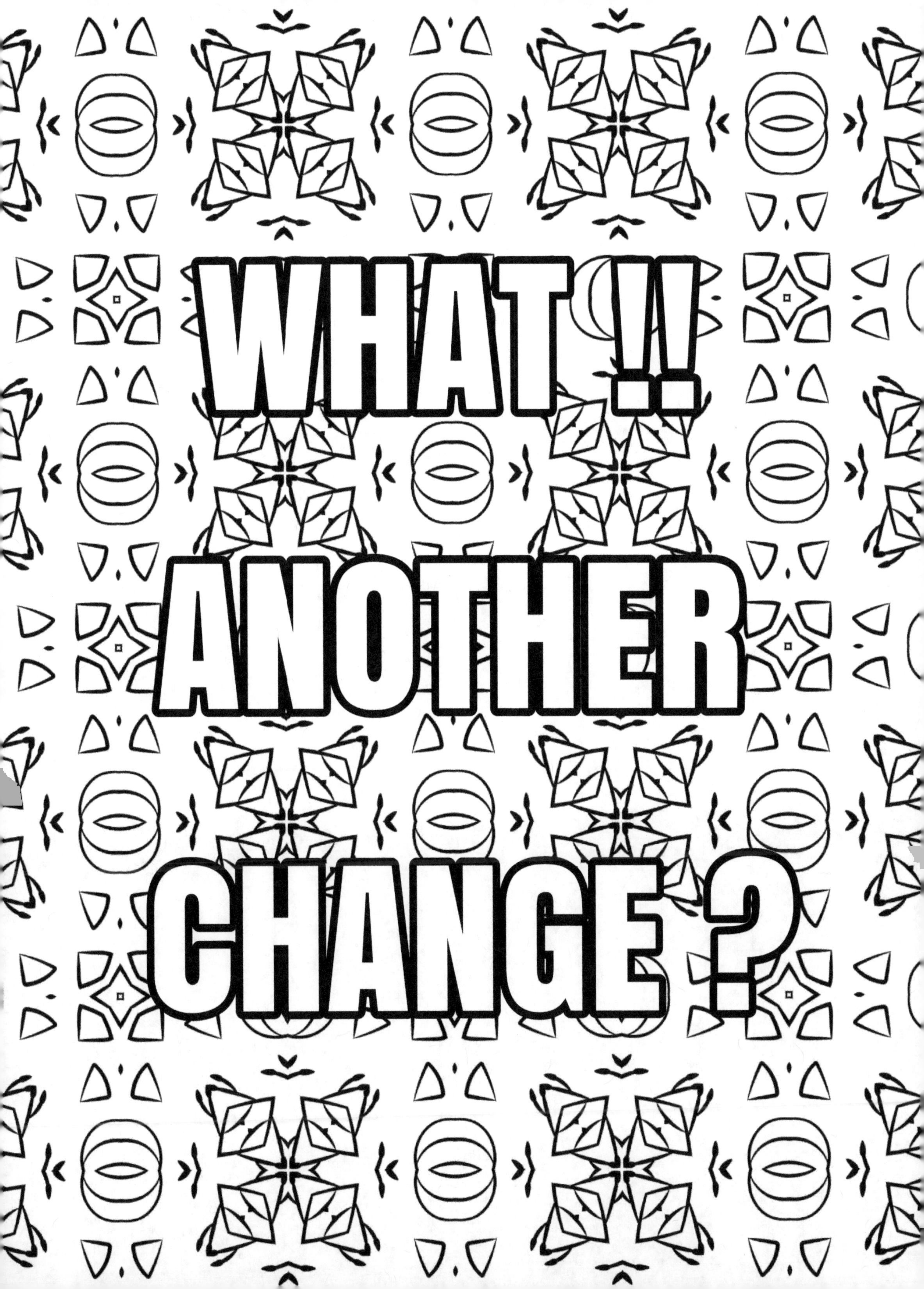
WHAT !!
ANOTHER
CHANGE ?

ANOTHER
LONG
STAND UP

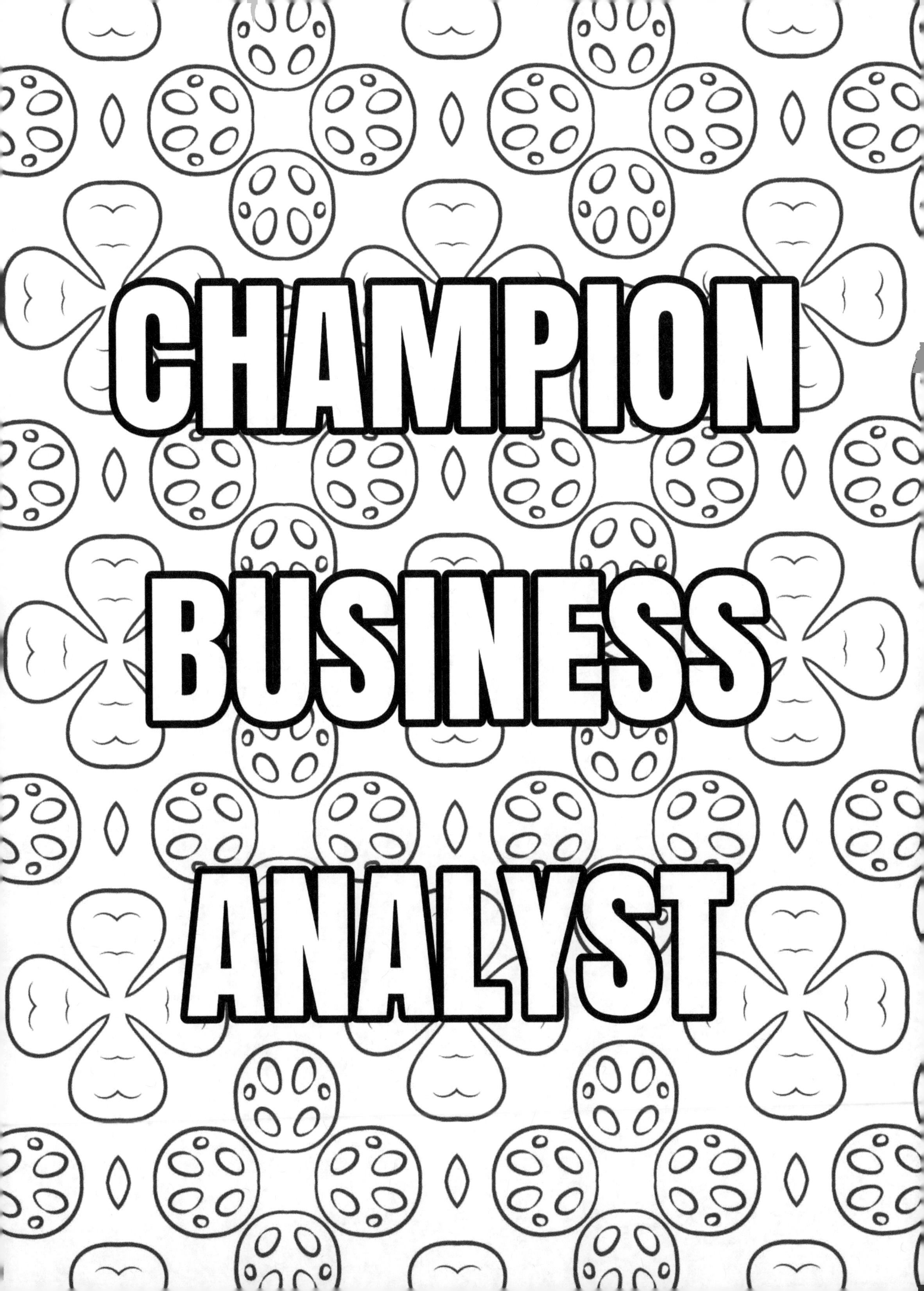
CHAMPION
BUSINESS
ANALYST

OH HE CALLED IN SICK

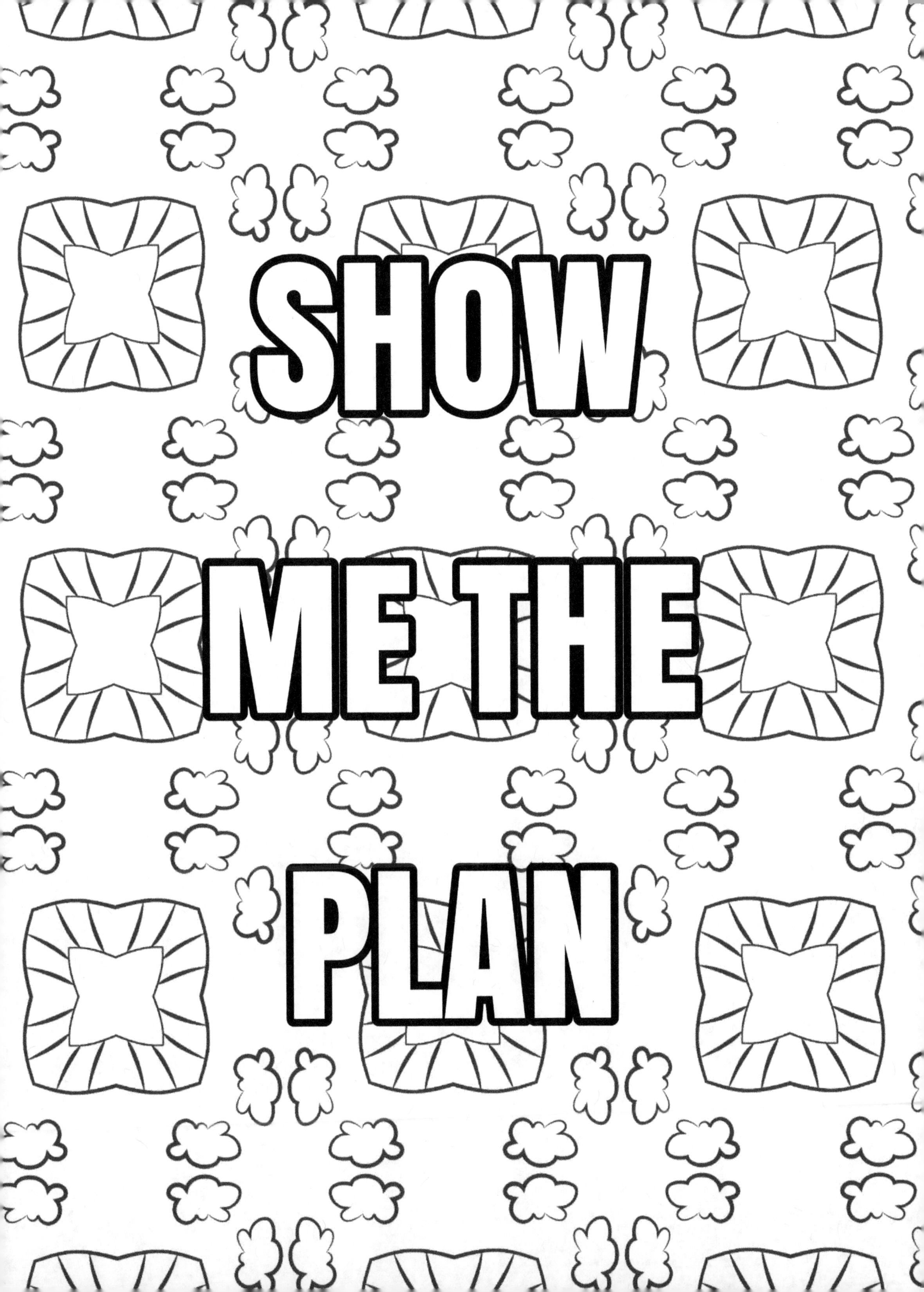
SHOW
ME THE
PLAN

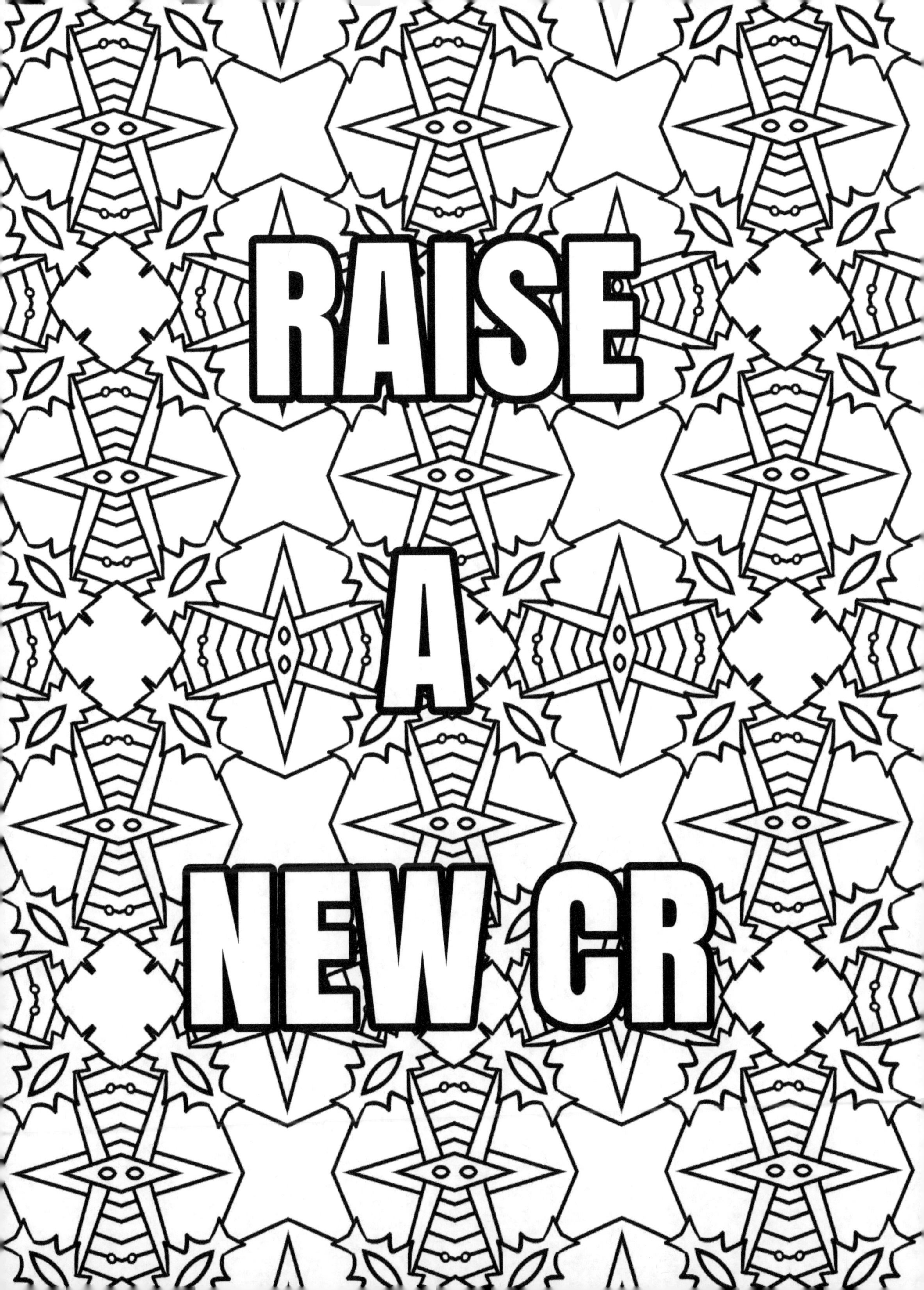
RAISE
A
NEW CR